Contrabassoon Method

ÁLVARO NOBRE MACHADO

ISBN-13: 979-8-9882334-1-1

Editing: Erik Piazza
Cover Design and Interior Layout: Lauren Woodrow
Cover Image: Dn Br/Shutterstock

Table of Contents

Preface

I started my contrabassoon journey without a contrabassoon teacher. A few years later I was tremendously fortunate to have had the chance to study with Simon van Holen in Amsterdam, from whom I have learned immensely.

During those years studying in Amsterdam, I reflected on how much faster I was improving and progressing as a player with his presence and his deep knowledge of the instrument and how to play it. More than that, technical difficulties (like cracking notes) that had no explanation before, became easy to fix with his guidance. This made me curious about how people experience the beginning of the contrabassoon approach, so I did extensive research. I investigated how some of today's professional contrabassoon players started their contrabassoon studies, available contrabassoon method books, and the challenges of playing the contrabassoon. I decided to write what I had not found written yet.

This book represents what I wish to have had in my hands when I started to play the contrabassoon some years ago. The purpose of this book is to be a guideline for learning and practicing the contrabassoon (rather than a school book in which one works on two pages a day) for students who may or may not have a contrabassoon teacher. There are exercises, technical aspects, and advice that is suitable for beginners, advanced players, and professionals alike. I leave it up to you to determine what to practice and how. With the contrabassoon, as with any other instrument, you are your own primary teacher. The amount of hours you spend with a teacher are a small fraction of the hours you will spend practicing, studying, and improving. You must always listen to yourself.

In this book, I will make a few claims and some indications of features that suit or do not suit the contrabassoon. These are not meant as a fact or absolute truth; these are mere recommendations. Moreover, they mostly refer to music written prior to the twentieth century. The aesthetic conceptions and instrumental playing paradigms have changed through time. Some music written in a later era may demand a different way to play the instrument (extreme articulation or kind of sound). Naturally, some may have alternate opinions to those presented in this book—it is through such passionate consideration that music continues to evolve.

To all the players who may use this book, I wish you all the best.

Álvaro

Acknowledgments

The writing of this method would not have been possible without the scholarship of the Gulbenkian Foundation in Portugal and the invaluable teaching of Simon van Holen, who besides sharing his immense knowledge, always demanded utter musical beauty from every note I would play on the instrument. To my family, friends, and Ricardo Ramos, sincere gratitude for the unwavering support and inspiration.

PART ONE

BASIC CONSIDERATIONS

The Contrabassoon, in Context

The contrabassoon has the lowest range in the woodwind section and often plays the lowest notes in the orchestra.

Due to its large range and richness in color and timbre, the contrabassoon plays together with every section of the orchestra. It blends splendidly as an extension of the string section, with the low brass (even with different notes, such as in chorales), the woodwinds (as the base of a great pyramid of sound in chords and melodic counterpoints), and even with the timpani. This is done in conjunction with building the sound-bridge between two of the aforementioned. This feature represents for the contrabassoon a very diverse and interesting role in the orchestra. It also demands a good insight of who we are playing with, as well as the ability to produce various timbres and colors besides articulation and dynamics. Bassoonists must develop these skills so they may better contribute and adapt to any musical scenario.

Brahms' *First Symphony* is an excellent piece to illustrate the different roles of the contrabassoon. The symphony starts with 8 bars of 3 different instrumental sections playing unison low C quavers (eighth-notes): timpani, double basses, and contrabassoon. In this place, the articulation and firm presence of the contrabassoon makes the bridge between the concise bluntness of the timpani and the throbbing tenuto of the double basses.

In the beginning of the "Allegro" the contrabassoon plays in unison with the double basses. Here we can help the bowed string sound beam become more "concrete" by playing with a fair amount of air and with a dark timbre. In doing so, we bridge the sound between the double basses and bassoons (which play a similar line one octave higher), blending these lines into one rich, thick sound beam.

In the fourth movement, there is a famous trombone chorale played twice—in the end of the slow introduction (pianissimo) and in the coda (fortissimo) with an orchestral tutti. In fact, both of these chorales feature the contrabassoon. The contrabassoon must be thoroughly attentive to the trombones—how long and the style in which they breathe, when and how they start a note, when they end it—and follow them accurately. The first time has a solemn character and soft dynamic; we should play accordingly. Not too soft but with a noble blending color. Later, exalting the same theme, it must complement the resonance of the fortíssimo trombone trio with a large amount of air and may dare to try a brighter color, always aware that a contrabassoon can outshine the trombone trio, though this should not be the desired result. Thus, one must project enough to contribute to the whole, but refrain from using too much tongue or from playing too loud or bright. This could turn a noble passage vulgar, producing a sound which is out of the core and character of the piece.

These are just three moments in the symphony, but every note that a contrabassoon plays in the orchestra has a clear and relevant purpose and it is important that the player knows that purpose in order to contribute to the best orchestral sound possible. The right intonation, timbre choice, dynamics, and articulation are fundamental points to achieve this.

With such a complex role, simply being able to play the instrument shouldn't be the ultimate challenge. We must learn to control the instrument and produce the sound we imagine without technical limitations or instrumental handicaps. Only then can we be so attentive to others and to the music happening in the rest of the orchestra, that we might contribute as the contrabassoon is designed.

Therefore, you must spend significant time getting to know the instrument in great detail before performing. This way, you can focus on musical expression and creativity when the time comes to perform.

Posture

Every individual has a different height, chairs are not all the same, and contrabassoons can be very different from one another. For these reasons it is very difficult to state one good way to sit and play the contrabassoon. Ergonomically speaking, there is no perfect way. You must consider many factors: how you sit, whether both sitting bones (ischial tuberosity) are equally supported on the chair, how diagonal the contrabassoon is, the height of the contrabassoon, how you distribute the weight of the contrabassoon, how you sit with the contrabassoon in order to see the music stand, the conductor and the first bassoon, etc.

It would be more ergonomic to sit symmetrically, with an imaginary line from the shoulders to the knees and the feet. In ideal conditions, these would be parallel, with a straight neck and no tension in the shoulders.

The contrabassoon stands on a spike that touches the floor and has a considerable weight falling to the left side of the player's body. It is healthy to let that weight fall on the left thigh instead of the left hand. The thigh is where we feel it the least, and will help us avoid the wrist pain or tendonitis that may develop from playing with such a weight on the wrist. Depending on the spike of the contrabassoon, you may or may not need to use your right foot to prevent the contrabassoon from moving. Although this is common among contrabassoon players, there is a healthier solution: attach a strap from your lower abdomen to the central metal ring near the right hand keys.

Keep your shoulders relaxed, especially the left one, as most contrabassoons are manufactured with the key work rather high in the instrument. This causes a tendency to raise the left arm. To spare the left shoulder, find the location on your left thigh where the instrument makes a right angle with the floor.

Maintain a right angle with both knees. For this, not any chair will work. The chair or stool should be rather low and then the height of the contrabassoon spike should be chosen carefully so that with the knees naturally bent, the neck can be completely relaxed in the most natural position. Sit nearer the front edge of the chair rather than the back.

It will take time to find your optimal posture. It is important that it is as natural and comfortable as possible. Always bring the instrument to you instead of moving the neck towards the instrument. It is always helpful to play in front of a mirror.

Breathing and Support

With good posture, you will be able to conquer some of the more difficult aspects of learning a wind instrument: breathing and support. A large part of the breathing mechanism is not as visible as the fingers or embouchure. Even tonguing, which is not visible, can be audible in a very evident way. This being stated, it is demanding for any teacher to understand what is happening with each student and it can be complicated to explain the process. The first instrument one must learn to "play" is oneself; therefore practicing should also have a component without the instrument.

Breathing and support are very important components of playing a wind instrument and it is easier to achieve and improve when one has a clear idea of how it works and how it should be investigated.

Although breathing in and out is one of our first instincts, playing an instrument demands a unique control over breathing. Contrabassoon players need to make the air travel through roughly six meters of tube in order to produce sound. Ergo, one should exercise breathing often.

Exercise:

1. Stand with your feet parallel to your shoulders and with the most natural posture possible, as if you just walked towards a mirror and started breathing.

2. Breathe out actively; exhale until the lungs are completely empty. Then, blow a bit more air until there is an empty feeling in your chest.

3. Relax and breathe in passively. Allow the larynx, lungs, abdomen, and torso muscles to work in full harmony as they were primitively designed, without "conscious thought."

4. Breathe in and out in a calm, relaxed and natural manner.

5. When you breathe in, your shoulders shouldn't rise; the chest shouldn't go up and forward immediately. Breathe deeply, down to the bottom of the backbone. Feel the expansion in the belly sides and lower back. Only then should you allow the chest to expand slightly.

6. After a few breathing cycles, while paying attention to the organic physiology of the exercise, you can start focusing on speeds and amounts.

7. With a metronome set at 60bpm, breathe in to full capacity in 4 beats and exhale for 4 beats as well. Calculate the air capacity in order to have organic inhalations and exhalations. If you start breathing in too fast and are almost at full capacity before it is time, there will be no space for more air in the last breath, just blocked body tension. The same will happen while blowing out (leading eventually to coughing). Therefore, it

is important to get to know your air capacity, and it may be helpful to start slower than you end. Think of a crescendo in the air amount during the breathing in, and a gradual increase of abdominal support with an increase in air amount breathing out. After a few successful cycles, change the proportion.

8. 3 beats in, 4 beats out; 2 beats in, 4 beats out; 1 beat in, 4 beats out.

9. Then, increase the exhalation time. 4 beats in, 5 beats out, 6 beats out, 8 beats out, etc.

10. At last, repeat steps 4 through 9, but with a "dSSSSSSS" sound while breathing out.

This "dSSSSSSS" sound is produced by slightly separating the teeth and placing the tongue behind the upper teeth. In order to produce this sound, you must breathe in and prepare the support. Just when the air is about to switch direction with the tongue, give the final release. This "SSS" sound takes less air (unless is done very loudly, which can be of help in an advanced stage), but needs huge abdominal support and provides great strengthening. The higher the pitch of the "SSS" sound, the more support you will need to use.

Exercising different air amounts and speeds while breathing in and out can expand air storage and increase the support capacity, which are both crucial for playing the contrabassoon (and bassoon).

Basic Instrument Care

In the lower vent of the instrument, near the right thumb key work, there is a removable pump which contains the water that condenses from the air we blow in the instrument. In that pump there is a key that opens a hole through which the water can be emptied. It is wise to remove it at the end of each day, or practice session. It is also a good idea to store the instrument with the pump in a separate pocket of the case so the instrument can "breathe" and dry better.

Common Mechanical Issues

Unfortunately, contacting a specialized contrabassoon overhaul expert is not always easy or cheap. When the instrument has a problem and there is no one around to help, there are a few things you could try. These common solutions should always be supervised by a bassoon teacher, at least. Ideally, these would be done by experts.

The most common problems with contrabassoons that are old and not played often (as for example, from some music schools) are difficult low notes, keys either too loud or stuck and hard to move, and broken bocals.

Low notes that don't respond are usually caused by leaks. This can happen due to incorrect tension in the key that holds the pad connected to that note, or the pad becomes too compressed and thin over time. The easiest and safest way to minimize this problem is to envelop the pad circle with ungummed smoking paper. That will help, temporarily, to close the gap left open by the old pad. Checking the tension in the spring may break the spring, causing a greater problem, therefore, I don't advise students to try this on their own. This can also be caused by small leaks in the wood or difficulty in getting the whole instrument to vibrate. For that, the only remedy is to play and get it vibrating again, to "get the instrument back to life."

Loud or stuck keys are usually caused by incorrect screw tension and/or oil that is too old or of insufficient quality. If they are loud, this usually means they are too loose. Taking the keys out, replacing the oil, and then putting them back again is quite complicated to do, especially for a student alone. I would suggest tightening the screws of those keys slightly, but not too tight that they don't easily move both ways. If some keys are stuck this means they are too tight or the oil has swollen and become dry. Replace the oil within each screw and key, or ideally have this done by a professional. If a student is reading this, the safest and easiest option is to try to slightly loosen the screws connected to that key. Just until the key moves again.

Broken bocals can usually not be fixed without a professional, who could seal the cracks. But if it's a cut along the neck of the curve, the easiest possible solution for a student, when there is no way to bring it to a professional, would be to wrap the whole section of the bocal very tightly with duct tape. This bocal will still work terribly, but it may become playable.

I sincerely hope you never have to deal with this without a specialized teacher or overhaul expert, who would fix all of this easily. But if you do, be very careful. Nowadays it is also possible to just post pictures of the issue on some social media groups and there will be several contrabassoonists ready to help. Contrabassoonists are very friendly with each other online (and in person)!

Maintaining the Wood

Not everybody agrees on how to maintain the wood. In every climate and region people have different tendencies for how often and how much oil to use on the wood. What I would suggest would be to contact an overhaul service provider and follow their advice, or even have them do it. If there is no access to one, I wouldn't risk anything unless advised by a bassoon teacher.

Swab

The best swab to use on the contrabassoon is a bassoon wing joint swab. After playing, you should pass it from the place the bocal goes and out the same place where the pump comes out. This will also make it safe to store it horizontally.

Reeds

This would be a vast enough topic on which to write a whole book, or series of books. I believe there is no perfect way to make reeds. For every way of blowing, embouchure, instrument, type of cane, and desired sound (color and sizewise), there are ways to make reeds and strategies on scraping them. In my opinion, one must make choices based on the balance and response of the reed. Consider easiness for soft dynamic articulation, dark sound in strong dynamics, tuning, stability, and colors in the high range, etc. Sometimes we have excellent reeds made from fantastic cane which provide us with an optimal balance, making us feel invincible. For various reasons this does not always happen.

What I can honestly say about this is that one should approach contrabassoon reeds the exact same way as bassoon reeds and scrape them with the same strategies as one would with bassoon reeds. Naturally, with time and practice this will change and we see differences, but that would be my starting point.

PART TWO

LEARNING TO PLAY

Introduction to Playing the Contrabassoon

If you are starting your contrabassoon journey with this method, welcome.

With attention, commitment, and patience, anything can be achieved with the contrabassoon.

Whether you started playing the contrabassoon because of some orchestra project or as a deliberate initiative, you must get to know the instrument and how to play it before you focus on some piece or excerpt. In any case, the chapters of this method are organized and ordered according to my taste of priority: first the basic rules, then learning how to make the instrument play the notes you want, then the way you want. However, you should work through these chapters in any order.

I encourage you to first take a look at the texts from each chapter, and work through these chapters in the order that best suits your needs.

If you have never played the contrabassoon before, the simplest way to start is to play a few slow chromatic scales in a short range and then in the range of one octave. For a few sequences, fingerings will be the same as the bassoon and you can concentrate on how different the physical feeling is while blowing into this instrument. (The dynamics exercises are very useful, and will help you learn to play with good air support.)

Later on, you should check the fingerings and slowly play through the following exercises. I recommend you play silently once, without blowing on the instrument—only moving the fingers on the keys while visualizing the notes before playing out loud. This way you can focus on the mechanical movements between each note at least once.

This should be done in a calm, patient, and confident manner. After a few correct movement sequences, you will be used to the fingerings and be able to play it with less and less effort.

However, fingerings should not be the primary concern in playing the contrabassoon. Fingerings are one of the first milestones, but you should spend time perfecting the various exercises in this book so you can improve the numerous skills needed to play the contrabassoon.

Technical Exercises

To get acquainted with the fingerings, as well as the air difference between each note, chromatic scales are very useful. (See the comprehensive set of fingering diagrams in Appendix B.) Playing each and every note within the octave, changing the key gradually will give our fingers innumerous repeated movements and sequences. This helps our brain store, imprint, and absorb the information so that later all these fingerings are immediately accessible. It is important that this is done slowly.

Chromatic Scales

Chromatic Scale – Exercise 1

Focus on air, the physical feeling, and how the sound is produced. Play slowly.

Chromatic Scale – Exercise 2

Check fingerings and play slowly.

Chromatic Scale – Exercise 3

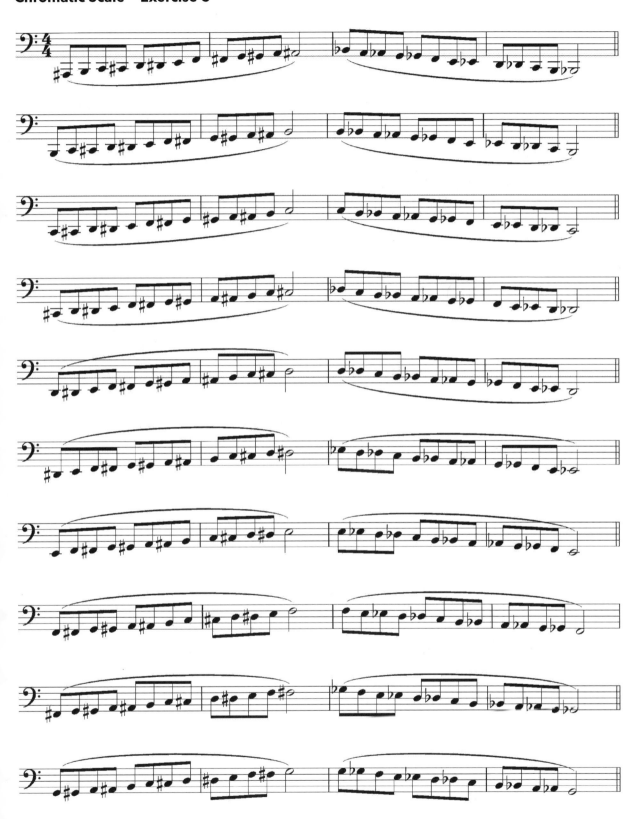

Chromatic Scale – Exercise 4

Before proceeding, it is good to repeat the previous exercises again, slowly.

With difficult passages, it helps to practice a sequence of notes with the fingers without properly playing—without the reed in the mouth—just moving the fingers looking at them and being aware of each movement. Then play. This way, you may spare some of the brain capacity that you would be using for the air, support, and blowing, and focus solely on the fingers.

Chromatic Scale – Exercise 5

When practicing the higher register, it is important not to disregard the rest of your playing. Keep a balanced sound, steady air column, and avoid biting to reach the high notes. Slow practice is the key for efficient learning.

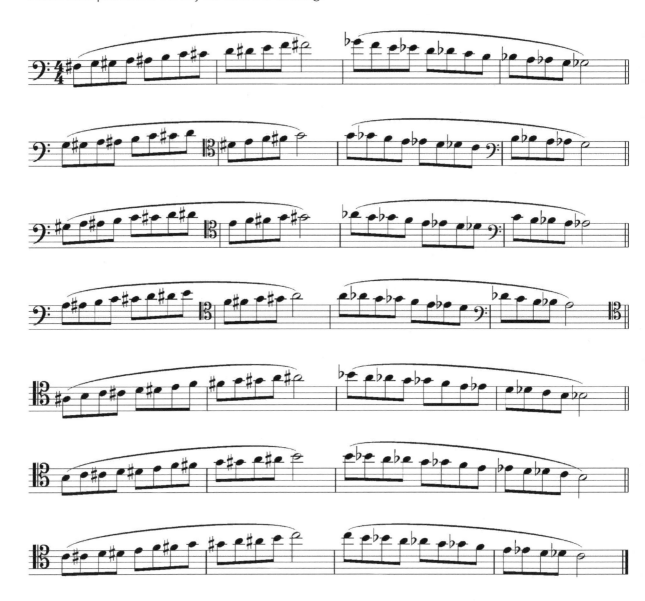

Chromatic Scale – Exercise 6

Feel free to keep going as high as you wish

Feel free to start as high as you wish

Diatonic Scales

For this I chose to keep the accidentals on the scales. Most players learn rather early which notes are sharp and which notes are flat in each tonality and, ideally, can practice scales without reading. Nevertheless, when learning fingerings, the purpose is to repeat correct movements and sequences. This conditions the brain to convert certain visual stimuli (notes written on a score) to a movement (a fingering, which will in most cases be different than the one we use for the bassoon, ergo, a deeply complex process). For that, this stage requires more detailed visual information than the usual key signature.

The patterns used in major mode and minor mode are different for diversification; both can be transposed to the other mode.

Diatonic Scale Exercise 1 – Major

E Major (####)

B Major (#####)

F# Major (######)

Db Major (bbbbb)

Ab Major (bbbb)

Eb Major (bbb)

Bb Major (bb)

F Major (b)

Diatonic Scale Exercise 2 – Harmonic Minor

E♭ minor (♭♭♭♭♭♭ + D♮)

E minor (♯ + D♯)

F minor (♭♭♭♭ + E♮)

F♯ minor (♯♯♯ + E♯)

G minor (♭♭ + F♯)

G♯ minor (♯♯♯♯ + F𝄪)

A minor (G♯)

B♭ minor (♭♭♭♭♭ + A♮)

Finger Technique

The following etudes will help you work on the fingerings in every range of the instrument. They should be played at a speed in which you know exactly which fingers to move and how, between every note, so that every move is correct. This way, only good, correct muscle memory information is imprinted in our brain, making learning optimal and efficient—even if this means it will be played very slowly.

I believe when a passage is difficult, we should deconstruct it into simpler elements, get to learn and understand those elements, and then put them all together. In order to be able to play the notes, this is often necessary. One way to do this is to separate the notes from the rhythm, tempo, character, and dynamics, and just mechanize the movements we need to do in order to play them. I highly recommend that you play different rhythm schemes and slurs as practice. That is helpful in every technical passage you might find, be it an etude, an exercise, an orchestral piece, or solo work. It can work with the whole passage or by separating it into small parts. Just take four notes and play them with these rhythms and articulations (and/or others that may make sense to you).

If it's more than four notes, start with the first four, then second to fifth and so on, or just pick every four. It also works with only two, or even three making the fourth note the same as the second.

I suggest the following rhythmic tools and slurs (the slur sequences work with all the different rhythms), to be used not only in my etudes but in general for any passage you may find.

Rhythm tools and slurs

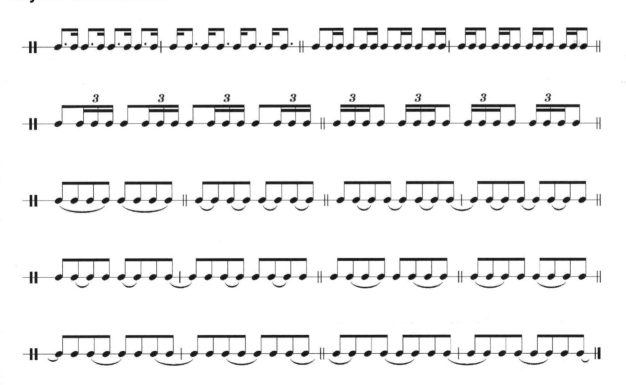

Etudes

Etudes on the middle register's fingerings

Leaps in the middle register, focusing on the left hand fingers and connection with surrounding notes.

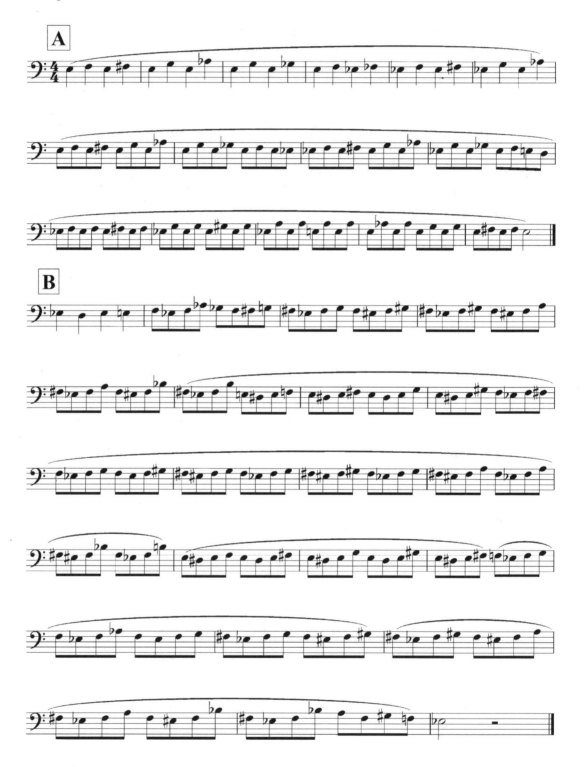

Etudes in the tenor register

Progressive leaps in the tenor register, focusing on the left thumb.

Mechanics around tenor C#

Advanced etudes for the left thumb and sensitive fingering sequences in the high registers

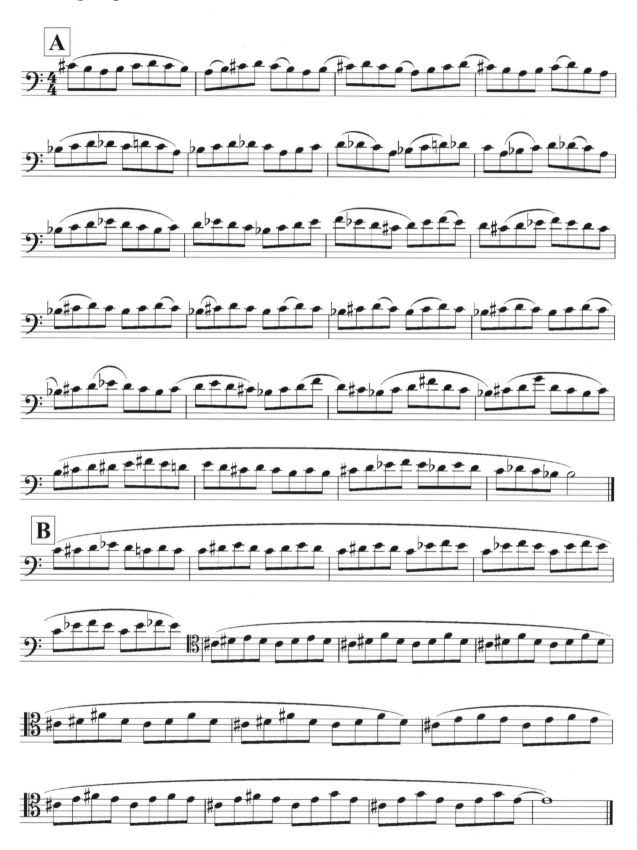

Contrabassoon Method

Articulation

What distinguishes spoken communication from animal vocalization is the articulation between vowels and consonants. When a child is born, its cries are initially vowels. Once a child articulates vowels with one or more consonants, a first word has been spoken. Clear and rich articulation is one of the most important stylistic and technical resources in playing a musical instrument.

Articulation is one of the most difficult things on the contrabassoon. Herein lies the biggest difference from the bassoon, and therefore our biggest challenge.

Every note has a beginning and an end. The beginning of each note should be clear and well "spoken" but the use of the tongue should be as little as possible. Speaking in mathematical terms, every note must be approached with at least a 70% air to 30% tongue proportion. With the right amount of air support and speed, any note can come without tongue. Then, the tongue simply gives the initial definition to the note.

Knowing this—and taking into consideration that accented, tenuto, staccato, *fp*, *sfz*, etc., all must start differently—the air and support needs to increase at least as much as the tongue attack on the reed. Failure to do so may cause the contrabassoon to sound like a percussion instrument in which the tongue is the mallet, an unfortunately common mistake.

You should be able to disassociate the use of the tongue with the dynamic. The same note can be approached with the same kind of tongue attack both in pianíssimo or fortíssimo; the air amount and support changes, not the tongue. A soft note still needs clarity and a loud note still needs to sound in the core of the instrument and without a crack. You must change the way you tongue the reed for a specific note if the intent is to start the note either with more or less consonant diction, not because the note is softer or louder.

The way a note is tongued should not be affected by its length or dynamic. However, the length of a note should be consciously related to dynamic in certain cases. The louder and more outspoken notes should not be too short; it is not an option that suits the contrabassoon as well as it suits other instruments. Furthermore in long notes, the support must increase while you are reaching the end of each note in order to keep the intonation.

The end of each note (when not followed by or inserted in a legato) should usually fade out. Depending on the speed, dynamic, and context of that note in the phrase—and of course if the contrabassoon is playing with different instrument(s)—that fading out will be longer/shorter or slower/faster. You should never stop a note's sound with the tongue. The result of that in a contrabassoon is very unmusical and in an orchestral context will fail to blend and contribute to a rich harmonic sound and articulation.

Given the fact that we mostly play with double basses and cellos, it is important to understand that no string player will block the strings vibration with their bow (the same way they start it) after they play a note. After they release the bow from the string, it still resonates inside the instrument, with its other strings, and through the hall even if they stop the string with their hand at some point. Although the wind instruments have no such feature, we must produce it artificially for music's sake. Thinking of a note as "Dommm" can be helpful; the "mmm" allows the end of the note to fade out organically. That fade out must happen through a strong increase of the diaphragm support as the amount of air blown into the instrument decreases. It cannot be achieved by biting for that would alter the color of the sound and tuning, as well as cause the reed to eventually close and stop vibrating. This would end the note at an unpredictable moment rather than when the player decides.

When in the orchestra, musicians should be aware of every little detail of the double bass and cello playing, since most of a contrabassoon's work in the orchestra is played along with these sections. A similar articulation means better blend, and ultimately a brilliant blend between strings and woodwinds, strings and timpani, etc. The contrabassoon can be a bridge between sections in an orchestra and a very well-adapted articulation is one of the keys to achieve that.

Knowing some facts about the string instruments will help the contrabassoon player to understand better how to interact with them.

When a string section starts a note of phrase with downbow, that means more diction and upbow means less. Starting near the frog has more arm weight which translates to more diction. Notes played nearer the tip of the bow will have less weight and will sound lighter. Finally, when they have separate notes played *portato* they will obviously be longer and *spiccato* shorter. It is good to observe that.

Working the articulation is a very delicate task and should be done with due concentration. For this, speed is of no help. One needs the time to fully prepare each approach to the reed consciously and to work the fade out.

Before any note or group of legato notes, you must at all times have the necessary amount of air in the lungs, the diaphragmatic support in place, the embouchure set, and the tongue on the reed. With the air and support in place, the note will start when the tongue is removed from the reed; the rearward movement of the tongue releases the air, never a forward movement of the tongue slapping the reed. Air produces sound in a wind instrument, not the tongue. The tongue is there to define the diction of the beginning of the notes and interrupt the air between notes or legato motives, nothing more. Every note can be reachable in any dynamic or articulation style.

Every note needs a different amount of air as well as air support and speed. Each note must be searched and known. One way to do it is to play each note a few times to get the physical feeling of the note. Then, play it a few times tenuto, then staccato in a comfortable mezzo-forte dynamic. After practicing this regularly for a few days, the brain will imprint the information and you will be ready to play the notes with the right air. Then, further work can start with broader dynamics and different tonguing.

Breathing for articulation

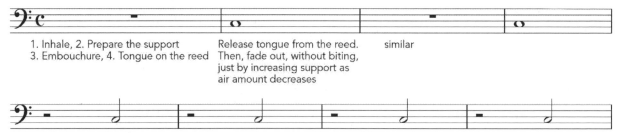

1. Inhale, 2. Prepare the support
3. Embouchure, 4. Tongue on the reed

Release tongue from the reed.
Then, fade out, without biting,
just by increasing support as
air amount decreases

similar

The four steps of preparation become faster

The previous exercise should be transposed to every note and practiced in different articulation styles and dynamics.

When you get to know each note of the instrument and are able to articulate different notes, speed may come. The same care and delicateness must occur for each note played, in all articulation styles and speeds.

Cracking Notes

For many players, cracking notes is one of the greatest challenges in contrabassoon playing, and the most difficult thing to overcome.

By "cracking notes," I mean notes that start with a noise usually similar to a crack, where one may or may not hear the desired note, but also several overblown harmonics.

With the wrong air-tongue proportion, any note can crack. However, several notes tend to crack more often than the rest on the contrabassoon. Knowing how to deal with the contrabassoon's characteristics and using the exact air-to-tongue proportion can help avoid cracking notes.

Cracking notes exist in two very close regions for different reasons.

The overblown F♯, G, and G♯ tend to crack very often in most contrabassoons, and in some instruments also the A. These notes crack on the contrabassoon because they are overblown without mechanical supplementation.

On the bassoon, those notes should be played with half hole using the first finger on the left hand (an important small technical detail that must be worked and perfected daily in order to get those notes without cracking both in legato and staccato). On the contrabassoon, all the fingers touch keys and not holes due to the big distance between holes that makes it impossible to reach. For this reason, the fingerings for the overblown F♯, G, and G♯ leave the left hand first finger hole open.

Contrabassoon manufacturers have tried to address this issue, dividing the first finger key into two pads (which open and close two holes). When we open this key but close the next one (F♯, G, and G♯), only one of those two opens. This measure helped stabilize these notes, but it didn't fix their attack. This causes cracks before the note speaks cleanly, and the crack is a cluster with harmonic overtones from that note.

The way to avoid cracking those notes and produce an optimal sound is to use significantly less tongue, and more air. If the contrabassoon usually requires a 70% air to 30% tongue proportion, these notes require at least a 85% air to 15% tongue proportion. In addition to this adaptation, you can help these notes by opening up the throat by lowering the larynx and oral cavity, as well as adding a slight weight on top of the reed to block the upper harmonics. This last technique should be worked in the mirror and not exaggerated; a scrupulously small movement will make the difference. It has to be as small and insignificant as possible in order to be able to change registers quickly both in legato and staccato.

To work this, you must first learn how much air to use and the physical placement of the tongue to give these notes their optimal sound.

Play each note a few times without tongue for a few seconds. Breathe in, then approach the note with a fast and strong *"H."* After accomplishing this a few times with a balanced sound, attempt to crescendo and diminuendo in tune. Once you can do this, play the same note more than once in one breath. At this point, you must breathe in and then *"H H H H,"* contracting the diaphragm for each note. When this is done right more than once, you will learn how much air and how fast the air must be for your instrument to reach a clean overblown F♯, G, and G♯. Then, start involving the tongue: first by alternating notes without tongue (*"H"*) with notes with tongue (*"D"*) and then by working the tongued notes.

For these notes, the search for the perfect spot in one's tongue is fundamental. When that point is found and mechanized, you will be able to play these notes at all times without cracks with different articulation styles.

Note: Every time *"H"* or *"D"* are mentioned in how to articulate certain notes, they **do not** refer to pitch names, but rather the use of the tongue.

Clean notes in the middle register

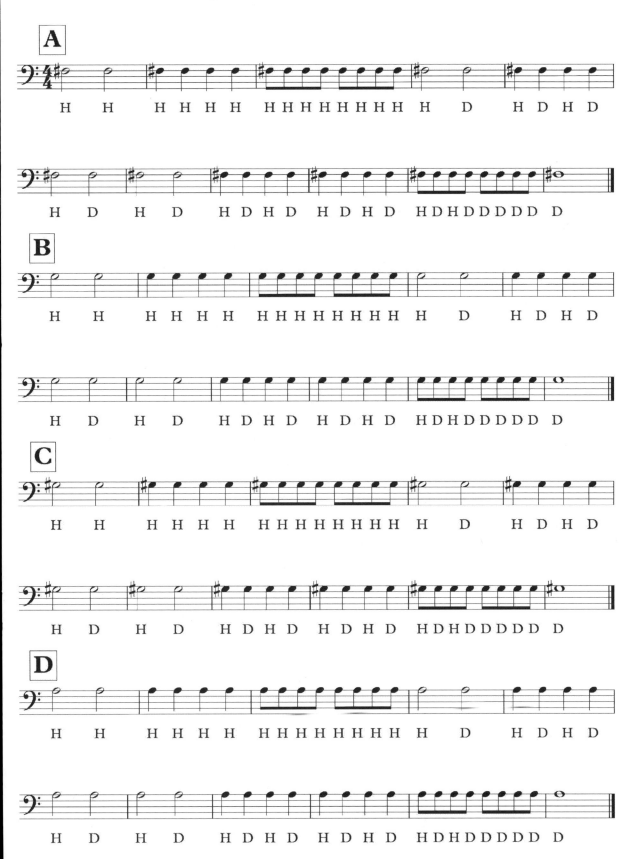

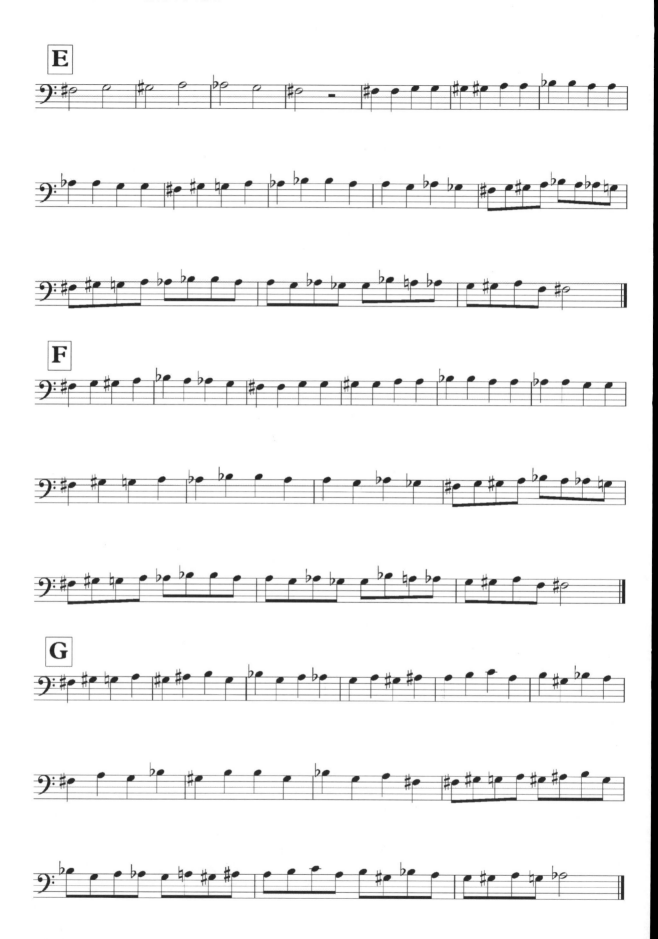

The other region is the tenor C# and D (in some contrabassoons, the C, B, and B♭ can crack, but C# and D are especially dangerous notes.)

While the bassoon has a whisper key with a different hole for B/C and a different one for D as well as a hole in the crook, the contrabassoon has two vent keys: the first is used until C# and the second from D upwards. On the most recent contrabassoon models there is a third one that helps with this, but most older contrabassoons don't have this. These notes are also overblown harmonics without mechanical proper compensation. Therefore, these notes need adjustment from the player.

To prevent these notes from cracking, a few fingerings can help but won't solve the cracking alone.

These notes are higher than the previous ones. Thus, they need faster air and even less tongue; 90% air to 10% tongue would be wise. The weight on the reed does not apply here. There must be no tension or force applied to the reed other than fast air.

Use the same procedure—playing without tongue. Play a few notes until you find the best, most open, and flexible sound.

Then, once more, alternate between "H D H D" articulations and find the optimal tongue spot. It might not be the same and it is likely that it will be more difficult to find.

Clean notes in the mid/upper register

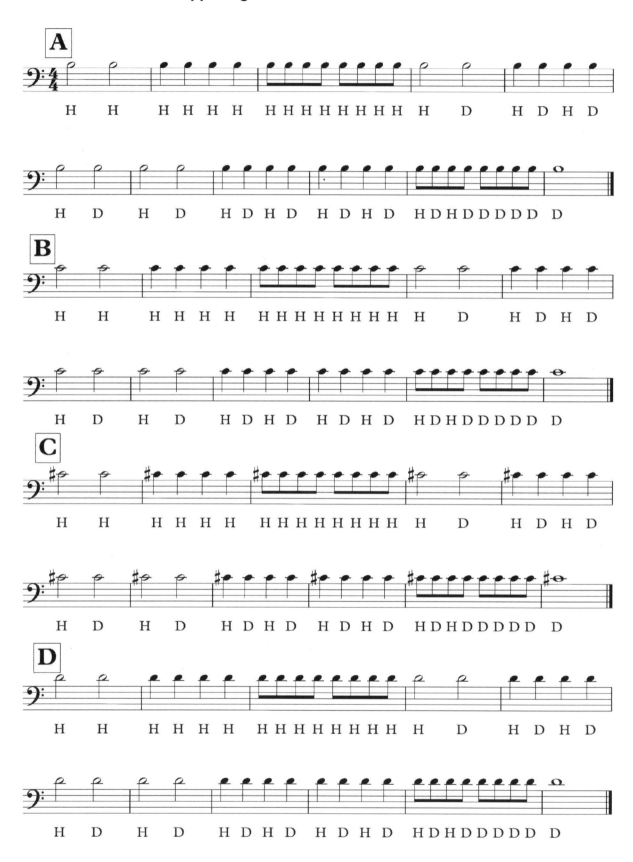

After you can confidently play a contrabassoon's tenor C, C♯, and D, you will need to combine the articulation of the F♯, G, and G♯ with the one from C, C♯, and D. Simultaneously, you must switch the chin's position, the fingerings, the tonguing, and the air support in order to produce all these notes with the correct intonation and the best possible sound. You may need a few weeks to figure this out. Work through these exercises very slowly, with patience and attention to all the steps.

Clean notes in-between registers

PART THREE

MAKING A BEAUTIFUL SOUND

Legato

In almost every language there is the diphthong and triphthong phenomenon, which happens when multiple vowels are joined. In English, examples of diphthongs include the words house and time. In German, *nein* and *auf*. Examples of triphthongs include the Spanish word *payaso*, the Italian word *maiale*, and the name of the country Uruguay.

When using diphthongs and triphthongs, the mutation between vowels is organically gradual, causing these to blend into one syllable alone, usually.

In musical instrument playing, legato is the phenomenon that happens when one note changes pitch as gradually and organically as with speaking; the result is one sound alone. One sound that at some point changes pitch, once or more than once. A properly produced legato is not as simple as just not tonguing. Legato demands exact change of fingers at the same time. With most notes, legato also requires a change of air amount and speed in a way that doesn't cause an obstacle in the sound or a color change between two notes. A beautiful and homogeneous legato is one of the most difficult but rewarding feelings one can have playing the contrabassoon.

There are three main tasks that need to be taken care of for a well-produced legato: precise fingers, air support, and sound color.

Precise Fingers

For a flawless legato, your fingers must be exact. When we slur between middle C and D only one finger moves, but with other intervals there is often the need to move more. When moving from middle E to F♯ or G♯, you must move 8 to 10 fingers. Therefore, finger technique must be precise, and for that it needs to be practiced slowly. It is as important to have a clean, smooth legato between notes in fast passages as it is between two very slow notes.

The following exercises are supposed to be played slowly with two things in mind. First, aim to always keep the embouchure loose. When relaxing it in order to get a low note, avoid biting for the next high note. This will result in the embouchure opening progressively—at some point you will have to find a balance. Second, the larynx should always be quite low and there should be room either in the throat or the embouchure to relax even further when slurring to a lower note.

A low larynx combined with relaxed and elongated facial muscles will enhance the resonance of our head's cavity, bringing a more natural amplification of the sound of the contrabassoon. Legato exercises also provide opportunities to work on sound color and projection through resonance rather than by pushing.

Air Support

You must be able to achieve any interval with the air and support without a gap between the notes but also without accenting the second note. For that, you should anticipate the note change in order to get the immediate sound when the fingers move.

Going upwards, you must anticipate the next note by increasing the support and air speed. Physically, this should feel like you are already playing the next note fractionally before the fingers switch it. By doing this, when you move your fingers, the transition is smooth and immediate.

Moving downwards, prepare to relax the embouchure and throat opening by lowering the larynx, but maintain steady support to keep the intonation. Before switching the fingering, you should already have the physical feeling of the next note while keeping the sound of the previous one.

This is difficult and takes a long time of slow practice to get to know how much to anticipate and adapt depending on each note. You must learn these subtle moves, adjusting support and embouchure, while maintaining precisely coordinated fingers. Work to automate these movements quickly enough to be able to do them almost constantly without changing tuning or color of the notes before the slur.

Sound Color

The contrabassoon, as well as the bassoon, has notes that are incredibly bright and loud where others are precisely the opposite. When slurring two notes, you must often play notes from those different groups together in the same legato phrase. You must find a common color for all notes in that slur (unless you want to empathize a specific note musically) that can be done by brightening up the darker ones, by shaping closer the brighter ones, or, in my opinion, ideally, bring both closer to your ideal color for that sentence.

This also takes time. You must be aware of the characteristic color of each note in order to compensate for the differences between each so that they all sound homogeneous.

Legato, support and flexibility exercises

All these exercises can and should be transposed to other keys.

Contrabassoon Method

Tone

From the earliest stages of learning an instrument, musicians should search for the best timbre possible. This means the sound must be balanced between the registers, consistent through dynamics, dark but defined, and round but broad. It should fill the hall and travel in space even in *piano*, but it shouldn't be nasal or bright even in *forte*. The sound of reeds vibrating against each other is something we do not want to hear.

The sound can be molded by the way one inhales and with the balance between air speed, amount of air, and the opening or closing of the throat (with the movement of the larynx). Tone is also affected by the relaxation or tension of the facial muscles, embouchure, and the point where the lips grasp the reed. Finally, the body posture, fingerings (in certain notes), and reed work together to create an ideal sound.

This ideal sound is achieved by a deep, "low pitched" inhalation through the mouth, connected to the use of a fair amount of air with very strong support, but without being tense or blocked and with a very low larynx. The facial muscles must remain as relaxed as possible. If one opens up the head cavity from the chin to the top of the head, with a vertical relaxed nose and lifted eyebrows, the sound gets even broader without pushing or breaking. Use a relaxed but supporting embouchure that grasps the reed not too far from the tip, as there is a point where the control over the vibration and sound is firmer. Biting at this point is not an option considering it would close the reed.

The reed defines the limits in the possibilities of one's sound. A reed that has matter (cane) to vibrate—with some tension between first and second wire rings and an openness that demands air from the player—will produce a bigger sound and be capable of more contrasts than a flatter thinner reed with less tension that plays effortlessly and will sound brighter but produce less volume. More cane in an open reed that requires more air will bring more vibration; less cane in a flat, easy blowing reed will produce brighter and sharper vibration, although less.

The right balance between a dark timbre and good projection is a constant search. It is very easy to have a very dark sound (with no considerable projection), and it is not really difficult to be very loud with a bright, broken sound. The challenge lies in being able to play with a sound that can fascinate any listener (sitting in any place of the hall) in every dynamic.

One way to practice this is to play a few intervals in the different ranges of the instrument. Practice crescendo and diminuendo, find the limits within the notes, and find the richest, fullest, most centered sound possible, as dark as your taste tells you. After you are in control of the sound and tone of the instrument, you can start exploring other sound colors. Then, by exploring sound colors, you also deepen your connection with the instrument as you learn different ways to shape the tone.

Sound Colors

One of the most fascinating features of the contrabassoon is its vast pallet of colors and possible timbres that are not always explored.

We like to produce our most beautiful sound, as we should. But we should also be aware that there is more than one possibility for a beautiful sound. There are several beautiful sound colors in the core of a contrabassoon, and each musical atmosphere and instrumental context has different needs. If not even the sky keeps the same color at all times, why must a contrabassoon? Many great musicians like to make nuances and contrasts with their sound color as much as they do with their dynamics or articulation. In the orchestra, while playing with different instruments and sections, this stylistic resource is particularly enriching.

To achieve a darker sound, open the throat, relax the embouchure and facial cavities, and maintain consistent abdominal support. To achieve a brighter sound, use fast air speed, a closed throat, a tighter embouchure, and contract the facial muscles. Different combinations of these aspects will alter the sound.

These should not be correlated to dynamics; "darker sound for *piano* dynamics and bright sound for *forte* dynamics" is not the idea. You should be able to play a dark, round, relaxed *forte* as well as a tense, bright *piano*. Controlling the different dynamics and colors of the instrument is absolutely necessary to be able to creatively choose when to play with which color.

The kind of tone, sound, color, or timbre that we emit when we play is transformed as much by each muscle of our body as by the instrument. In one end the feet of the player and where they stand, in the other the bell of the instrument resonating in the hall. Posture alters the sound, the kind of stage platform or mat the contrabassoon spike is at, the way the orchestra or group is displayed, and moreover the hall's acoustic alters the perception of this sound. Therefore, you must realize all variables and adapt.

When a contrabassoon plays with the double basses or in a full brass chorale, the timbre can be different. When there is a melody played only by contrabassoon and bassoon, the color doesn't have to be the same as in a contrabassoon and tuba melody. Once more, it is important to be aware of whom you are playing with. You must know if your sound must mingle into the other, rather than hosting the other (when sharing a melody a contrabassoon's sound can host the bassoon or english horn's sound, while on the other hand it should mingle into the tuba's). Even when this is clear, the instrumentation of the whole piece must also be taken into consideration.

A contrabassoon player shouldn't play Mahler's *Fourth Symphony* the same way as one would play the *Sixth Symphony*. The fact that the former has neither trombones nor tuba parts changes the role of the contrabassoon. Speaking of the *Fourth*, in the glorious or dramatic *forte* (and beyond) moments featuring trumpets and horns, the contrabassoon needs to bring backbone and strength to the double bass and cello section in order to support the whole orchestra's resonant *tutti*, without sticking out with too bright a sound. On the other hand, during the second movement's solo, the contrabassoon can just bring a touch of edge to the scene. If we discuss the loud moments in the "Finale" of the *Sixth Symphony*, the hammers, tuba, and trombones will bring the power to the group and there are far more double basses. The contrabassoon can therefore opt for a different sound than it would otherwise, whereas the contribution needed is different.

All these color choices come from the creativity and taste of the player. I don't intend to dictate how to play in certain groups, but rather to help provide the tools and skills to play with different timbres and be able to choose them according to each musical atmosphere and instrumentation.

The search for the colors of sound takes years and you can always be surprised. It is an exciting journey and you should always be open to experiment and learn more from time and the instrument itself.

A way to practice this skill can be to pick a theme or themes from a piece you are playing or have played, or even just a theme you like, and explore ways to play it in which you get different results, until you find the color you like the most. The more flexible you become with tone and color, the more creative you can be.

Tuning

Intonation is one of the main challenges and first noticeable skills in any wind or string instrument playing. It is a journey that a musician takes during the entire learning process and throughout their career. In this matter, a contrabassoon is not much different than any other instrument except for the fact that a contrabassoon player needs to discern deep low notes.

Tuning has two very important components: the insight and the playing. Both need to be worked in order to improve.

Intonation insight is basically how you perceive tuned intervals and sounds. This results in how accurate and demanding perception is with intonation. Each interval is optimized in your inner conscience by being heard and taken as correct from a reliable source. Listening to, for example, Mozart and Beethoven sonatas played on a tuned piano (most likely in tune on a good recording) are very helpful for the tuning insight as well as for harmonic clarity.

The musical ear needs to be trained to perceive the intervals and discern if this interval is in tune, either a horizontal interval or a vertical one. Horizontal intervals mean the tuning of successive notes played by the same player in a musical phrase; these should be a concern whether playing with other instruments or alone. Vertical tuning is the tuning between more than one note played at the same time by different players. Both need to be clear for the player.

Harmonic knowledge is extremely important in order to be in tune vertically. To know in which chords each note is, and which function each note takes in each chord is fundamental for accurate tuning. In the first few years you may need to check the key and see the chord progression that takes place in the piece you are playing in order to determine which function your note takes. With time you will recognize the chord progressions and the function of your note.

The player needs to be very critical spotting each interval and note, and have a very clear idea of how each interval should sound. When you know how to tune each note and how far from each other the notes are meant to sound, there comes the need for total control over the instrument. For that, a player must also know the instrument enough to know the place of every note: which notes are sharp, which notes are flat, and the dynamic limit of every note. Not all notes can reach the same dynamics without damaging the intonation; you must learn each note's peculiarities, tendencies, and limitations. Knowing this, you must control the instrument enough to be able to play any note or a musical phrase tuned as wished in any key, as well as flexible to the point where you can adapt to others and be in tune.

There are different ways to temper tuning. Woodwind sections often tune with pure intervals rather than well-tempered tuning as in a piano. In solo playing and practicing, it is common practice to be closer to the well-tempered tuning than to use just intonation, but depending on taste, a fair amount of players opt for just intonation in triad chords.

When it comes to just intonation, tuning perfect triads in orchestral woodwind sections is the main challenge. In this context, major thirds should be lowered approximately 14 cents, minor thirds raised by 16 cents, and perfect fifths raised by 2 cents. These are standard numbers but depending on certain schools and taste, they may be debatable. Balance is at least as important as tuning for this to work. First, it is advised that there is a sort of pyramid of sound, considering the bottom has a markedly pronounced resonance in comparison to the highest. Harmonically, the root (fundamental) should be the loudest note. After that, the fifth, and only then the third. A seventh functions as a third on the fifth.

These kinds of tunings and calculations are very useful for an orchestral player of any woodwind section. However, a contrabassoon player must understand clearly every harmonic scene in a piece and discern the function of every single note in the part in order to play it in tune and build up the right chord (which sometimes is inverted).

Any bassoon or contrabassoon player needs to have accurate tuning capabilities. Both instruments are harmonically misbalanced in their intervals, resulting in a demand for a very accurate player to tackle these handicaps and play in tune. The bassoon and contrabassoon (when playing together with other instruments and in the orchestra) are often the foundation of the harmony. Thus, the whole ensemble relies on the stability and support of the bassoons and contrabassoon and, ideally, builds chords from their notes.

Because the contrabassoon reaches such low notes, you must work the musical ear to the low frequencies and harmonics in order to be able to discern if certain notes are in tune. You must always be able to predict which exact pitch you wish to obtain from the instrument. This can be worked by practicing the contra sitting by the piano (sideways). Play the desired note on the piano pressing the sustain pedal with the left foot and then play on the contrabassoon aiming to match the tuning of the piano. This exercise is good for both unisons and for intervals.

Tuning Exercise

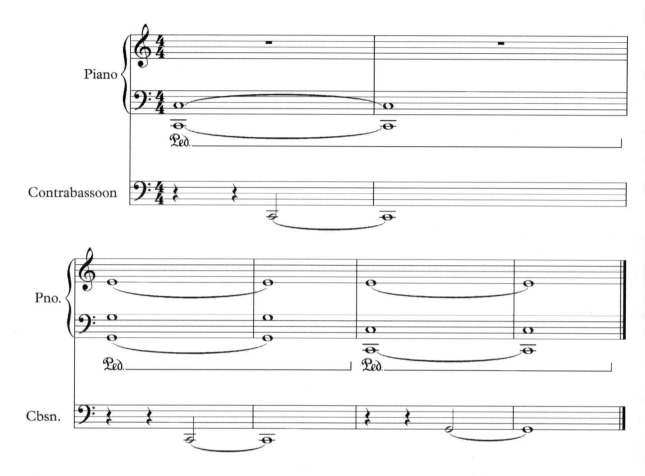

This exercise is transposable to any note and interval.

Dynamics

The use of dynamics is one of the cornerstones of music. Its use, along with crescendo and diminuendo, is one of the most primary ways of musical expression.

It's fundamental that dynamics are clear and contrasting enough without affecting the intonation or sound quality. Each note has a dynamic range and further that note's limit, beyond which the sound and intonation stability will be damaged. You must know the instrument in hand enough to handle the dynamics without damaging the sound and intonation of any note.

In a musical context, and especially in the orchestra, the dynamics do not always mean decibel amount, rather than being a matter of character and degree of intimacy or extroversion in the sound. Nevertheless, on a fundamental level, you need to know and control the instrument enough to pursue the dynamics in a literal way.

The sound produced by the contrabassoon should fill the hall with the same quality in any dynamic. For that reason it is important not to push the louder dynamics with a high larynx and unsupported air. Instead, use the resonance of the whole body to achieve a relaxed, full sound by lowering the larynx and matching support to the amount of air used. In softer dynamics, keep the harmonics in the sound and the air column flexible enough to allow phrasing. In order to succeed with this, there can be no biting or tension in the upper body. Less air must flow faster with increased support.

Crescendo should be achieved with the gradual increase of air. As the air amount increases, the throat must open and the facial muscles relax in order not to brighten up the sound or raise the pitch. The result must be a natural growth of the sound, rather than a pushing feeling.

Diminuendo works with gradual decrease in the amount of air, although the air speed and support should increase as one decreases the amount of air. At all times the embouchure must be as relaxed as the note allows, ergo, no biting. Otherwise, not only will the sound and intonation be affected, but the air stream might be blocked. A closed reed does not vibrate. The result of a diminuendo, for the audience, should be a feeling that the source of the sound is moving away from the listener, instead of choking or muting the sound.

For every crescendo and diminuendo, there are ranges and speeds. A player can expand their limits with the following slow exercises.

Dynamics Exercise 1

And so on...

And beyond...

Dynamics Exercise 2

Sound waves by steps.

(Repeat with different notes)

Dynamics Exercise 3

Sound waves by jumps.

PART FOUR

ADVANCED CHALLENGES

Opening the Highest Register

The highest register on the contrabassoon (between the high B natural and E♭ or even E), is not more difficult than on the bassoon. The challenge lies with the instrument itself rather than with the technique required to reach those notes.

The fingerings for these notes are quite simple, but most contrabassoonists do not play in this range. This area of the harmonics and vibration can be under-stimulated. Only with time and patience can you feel free and flexible in this register. It can take a few days.

When in non-legato passages, you should use absolutely no tongue or the softest possible touch.

At first, I recommend you use stronger, harder, or even shorter reeds to facilitate reaching these notes. After you are properly used to playing in this range, as well as the instrument, any regular reed will work. Slightly stronger tension and grip may happen, but avoid biting to reach these notes.

Register Exercise 1

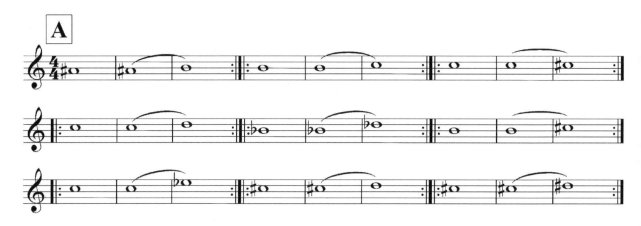

This should be practiced in a calm, attentive, and patient manner. It will take time and effort to open up these notes, and can take a few days with only a few minutes of regular work. Slow chromatic slurs starting from the high A are the best beginning. Only later should you work on approaching the notes from silence.

At first it can be difficult to make the C♯ sound. It can take days until it sounds but you should keep the same embouchure as with the C and previous notes and just keep blowing fast air. This is one of the most difficult notes to free in the contrabassoon. After that, a little more patience will also bring out the D and other notes.

Register Exercise 2

Only after this work is done can you proceed to the following chromatic etudes, which should be played rather slowly.

Register Exercise 3

Bassoon Form Recovery

At some point, you will get used to playing contrabassoon and achieve a feeling as comfortable and natural as with playing bassoon. Before that happens, you may already feel things changing on the bassoon, not all of which will help you.

As you may know, playing the contrabassoon is very different from the bassoon in such ways as air amount and speed, tonguing, embouchure, fingerings, posture, etc. For this reason, there are a couple of things you must do in order to switch back to the bassoon, ideally every day you play both instruments.

The following exercises have to be done slowly and progressively to pay attention to the differences between the ways you play each instrument. Even when you know how to play both instruments, the signals and stimuli that the brain will send to the fingers, diaphragm, abdominal muscles, tongue, etc. will not necessarily be the most intuitive. Knowledge is not always reflected in every movement, therefore we must insist on imprinting the right movements in order to get them as automatically as possible, as well as re-adapting to them every day.

For example, the contrabassoon has no finger-holes, therefore no note is played with half hole, just pressed key or open key. When you play contrabassoon often, the automation of the half hole technique is no longer being stimulated. As such, it may occur that while playing the bassoon later on, a passage with a G or A♭ will crack in that note because the half hole was not exactly as open or closed as it should be. The same way you must remember everyday how to tongue a G, Ab, C♯, and D on the contrabassoon, you must also remember how to half hole properly on the bassoon.

Bassoon Exercise 1

Bassoon Exercise 2

Bassoon Exercise 3

You must spend a long time getting used to each detail of playing the contrabassoon and the differences to bassoon playing. Only then will you master the switch between instruments that we so often need in various orchestral pieces as well as in auditions without having to do this whole adaptation exercise.

Playing with a Different Instrument

One of the struggles for contrabassoon players is frequently having to play on different instruments. For instance: in auditions abroad when it is not possible to bring the instrument we are used to playing on, in a youth orchestra, or in collaboration with a professional orchestra.

It can happen that the instrument that comes before us is the best we have ever played and just came from an overhaul. In that case, an easy task will follow, but this is not always what happens.

A player should be able to adapt to an unknown instrument, with its own peculiarities, its possible limitations, and potentialities. Also, expect the tuning and resistance of each note to potentially be different. The problematic notes and the general tuning should be the first two things to check when getting to know an instrument. Then, find the best fingerings for these problematic notes.

After exploring the tone, intonation, and problematic notes, check for cracks in the transition registers and the ease of legato.

This exercise will define how well you will adapt to a new instrument. Therefore, full concentration and physical shape come in order. It is best to first complete the warm up with the breathing and the bassoon. It is also good to have more than a few reeds in good shape. You might still have to scrape because every instrument has different demands.

It can take half an hour to two hours to get a full diagnosis of the instrument, depending on your experience and the state of the instrument. You need to discern what needs to be done to each note and the limits of each note. Be extremely focused—it may help to write down some aspects to have in mind to remind yourself before the first rehearsal or audition.

A professional contrabassoonist may start to feel completely comfortable after approximately 12 to 16 hours of playing. In an orchestral context, this might mean just before the first concert, in a good scenario. The more you play a new instrument, the faster you will feel comfortable with it and be able to express your musicianship through the instrument without worrying about its technicalities. That must always be the aim.

You must try the following exercises in order to get used to a new instrument. Only then should you start focusing on the excerpts and pieces about to be played.

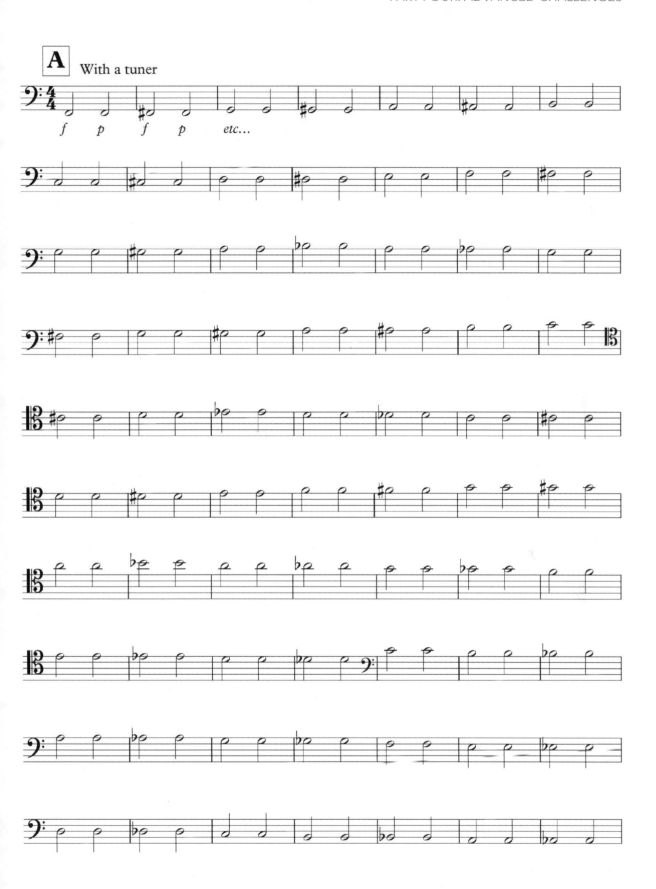

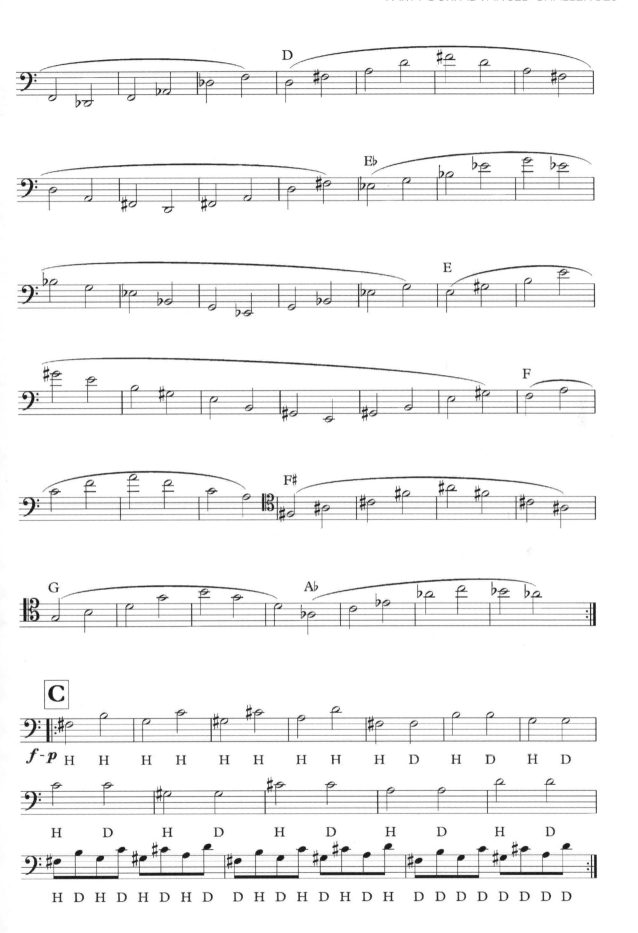

APPENDICES

Appendix A: Recommended Resources

The focus of this method is to help and guide contrabassoon players to get to know the contrabassoon and learn its fundamentals and skills. Given that most contrabassoon players (at least in my generation) don't have a specialized teacher at the beginning of the process, it is important to have good foundational information.

Il Controfagotto. The Contrabassoon, History and Technique
Inconis, Raimondo (2009)

> This is an excellent contrabassoon encyclopedia with a very accurate and detailed history and information about the contrabassoon's genesis, its repertoire, the mechanic evolution, and constructors. Furthermore, it has a list of all the pieces where the contrabassoon is featured until 2009. In addition to a solid theory basis, it has basic and advanced exercises, and finger agility drills, followed by a large collection of excerpts from orchestral pieces. This work also mentions posture, reed making, fingering charts, and trill fingerings.

Das Kontrafagott. Volume 6
Seltmann W. and Angerhöfer G. (1984)

> The first five volumes refer to different aspects of the bassoon, but the sixth volume is specifically for the contrabassoon. The sixth and last volume of the collection "Fagott-Schule," in a later edition "Das Fagott" is a source of precious information about the contrabassoon. The excerpt-based studies are, in my opinion, the most interesting feature, and are very useful for mastering orchestral excerpts.

25 Studies in Scales and Chords Opus 24 and 50 Concert Studies Op. 26
Milde, Ludwig (1891)

> These studies are a reference for the bassoon but are also very interesting for the contrabassoon, especially if you have practiced this book on the bassoon. The *25 Studies in Scales and Chords Opus 24* helps you get used to each tonality by practicing technical studies that have been worked on the bassoon once before. By working on something we know, we have worked on the bassoon before, we are not reading anymore, we know the notes, we learn to play those sequences and motives in the contrabassoon with the new fingerings and moves.

> The *50 Concert Studies Op. 26* is in my opinion a must for every player primarily because it is often asked for in auditions. Number 9 is most common, but others such as 28 or 49 have been asked for by professional orchestras. Furthermore, the studies from this composition are musically very interesting, that's why they are called concert studies; they can be performed in a concert. These are studies that although have a technical purpose (which is different in each study), have also an

artistic feature that takes an important part in the execution of the study. That brings a different challenge to the practice, considering you are not only working on the fingerings, air stream, flexibility, or articulation. You are making music through all these. Making music is the ultimate goal and these studies help you achieve that goal through the technicalities.

Numbers 9 and 10 are the two most important ones for me. Number 9 is a beautiful, deep, slow piece, focusing on legato and air stream flexibility, along with dynamics along a quite wide range. Number 10 has a different musical character with a lighter mood focused on articulation and staccato, and on the worst contrabassoon cracking notes with different intervals. When you can play both these studies, concentrating your energy and focus on musical phrasing and artistic taste, you can say you are in shape. These exercises are also very useful for fully mastering a preparation with a different contrabassoon.

.drills.
Dahl, Ole Kristian T. and Cameron Kaitlyn G. (2013)

This book can help you understand how logical the bassoon can be. It helped me learn that every technical aspect and feature of the bassoon can be embraced and learned through playful and logical exercises. Some of the "drills" and ideas (for example, the "drill no.1" and "the flex exercise") fit the contrabassoon very well.

BASSOON FUNDAMENTALS, A Guide to Effective Practice
Klütsch, Georg. (2003)

This guide is a source of technical exercises with very clear and interesting notions of tone, sound, and tuning. It also offers a vast bassoon trill fingering chart as well as finger technical exercises. I find this to be an excellent bassoon book.

Richard Bobo

The American contrabassoon player has already published some incredibly valuable resources online, in my time, specially related to fingerings, not only for notes, but also trills, multiphonics, alternative tunings and much more. Whenever he publishes more content, you should pay attention.

Appendix B: Fingering Diagrams

When learning a new language, we first learn vocabulary and grammar, and then relate these to the mother language. When speaking, we initially translate our thoughts and words from our primary language into the new language. We achieve fluency only when we can immediately think in the foreign language and express our thoughts without effort.

The same happens with the contrabassoon. In the beginning we relate everything to the bassoon and consider certain fingerings as "just like in the bassoon except for…". This is normal; it is how the human mind works, through association and relation. However, we become fluent in the contrabassoon when this is not happening anymore and the fingerings just come to the hands without hesitation or thinking. Fluency takes time and is a result of very slow practice. Do not attempt to learn all the fingerings at once. This process should be gradual and you should give your brain time to absorb all the information.

When practicing new fingerings, it is important (at least in the beginning) to use standard fingerings rather than having several for each note and not knowing when to use which. There are numerous fingerings for each note on the contrabassoon. I have included the fingerings I find work best.

I have indicated the primary fingerings in gray, the keys that help with intonation with vertical lines, and the keys that can be used if a particular note requires extra help to speak clean without cracking. The vertically lined keys help bring out some harmonics that help the note speak clearly with stable intonation. With regular fingerings, in some instruments, it is difficult to distinguish between certain notes (e.g., low F or F♯) due to the presence of all the harmonics and overtones. In most cases, all vertically lined keys are ideal. Every contrabassoon has particular intonation tendencies, and you may need to experiment to find the combination that works best on your instrument. Thus, every fingering with vertically lined keys added to it offers a group of combinations using some of the keys marked with vertical lines. You may need to omit some of those during fast technical sections with many notes (musical fluency is the priority).

The fingerings from the auxiliary section are the ones I use either for a darker color and smoother legato, for technical purposes in a fast moment, or for a more open sound without cracking.

Many more fingerings can be found easily online or in other books. Although I chose to compile in this book the ones that I use and find the best, everyone discovers new fingerings and new ways to do things. You will also eventually develop the fingerings that work best for you.

Key Diagram

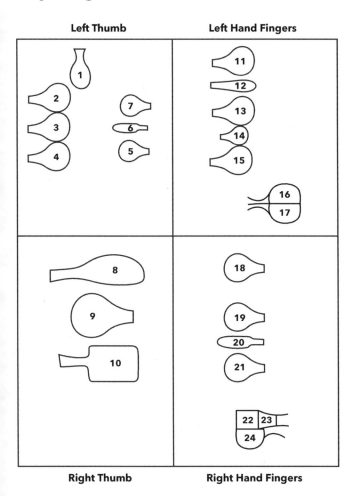

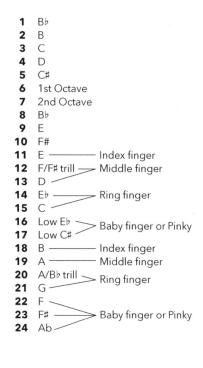

1	B♭
2	B
3	C
4	D
5	C#
6	1st Octave
7	2nd Octave
8	B♭
9	E
10	F#
11	E ——————— Index finger
12	F/F# trill —— Middle finger
13	D
14	E♭ ——————— Ring finger
15	C
16	Low E♭ —— Baby finger or Pinky
17	Low C#
18	B ——————— Index finger
19	A ——————— Middle finger
20	A/B♭ trill —— Ring finger
21	G
22	F
23	F# —— Baby finger or Pinky
24	A♭

 Gray - Primary keys

 Vertical lines - Tone and tune keys

 Black - Emergency keys

It is likely the contrabassoon in your hands has more keys than this, it can have an A♭ key next to the F# (10) key, an auxiliary E♭ key above 8 or 18 (sometimes both), a few extra keys in the left thumb area (an extension to the second octave key under the C# (5) key, an extension to the C# above the second octave (7) key, and even extra keys to help with the high notes. All these are useful for certain passages but first you must get to know the instrument and realize precisely what those keys are meant to do, especially on the left thumb. The keys in this diagram are the standard basic and using these you can get everything out of the instrument.

Standard Fingerings

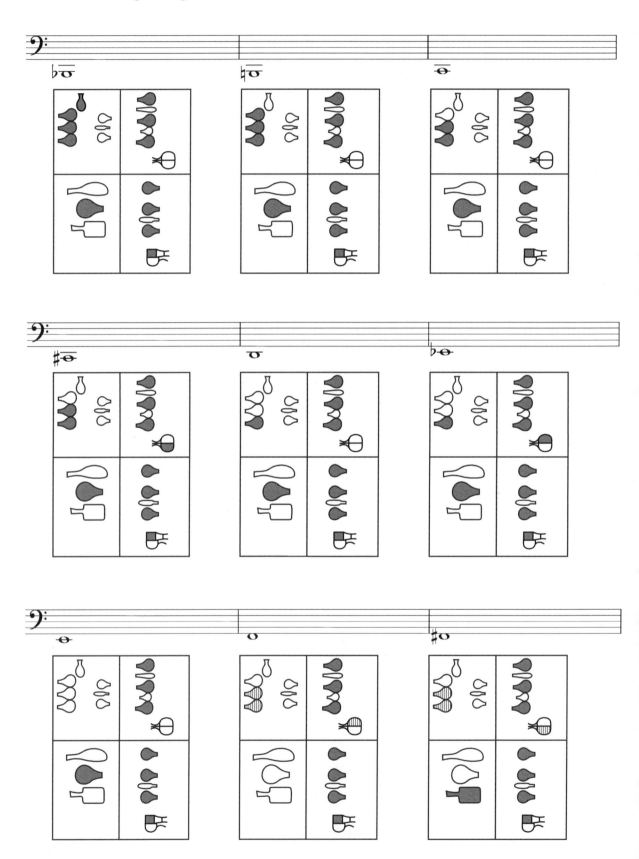

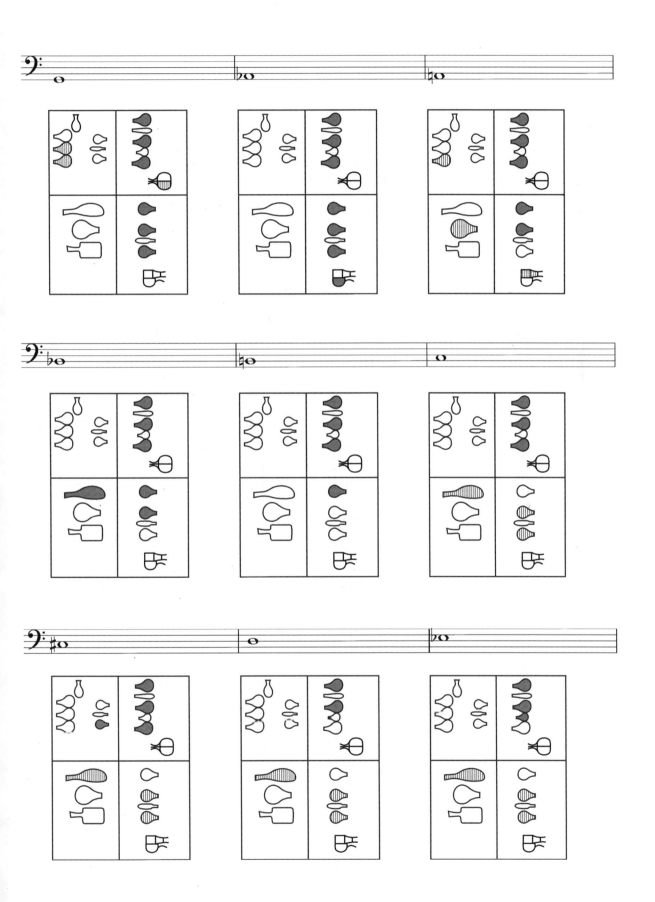

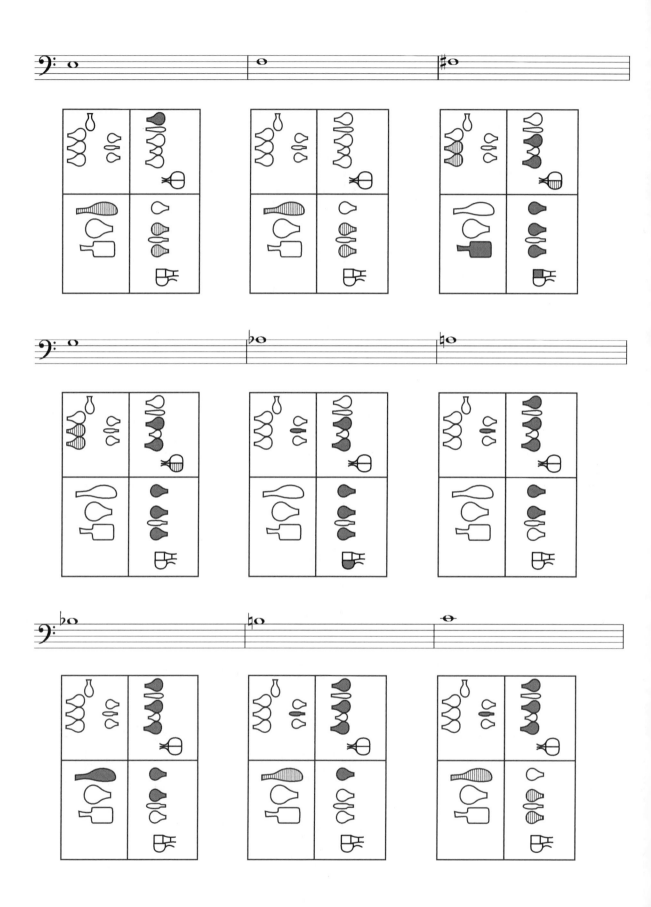

Contrabassoon Method

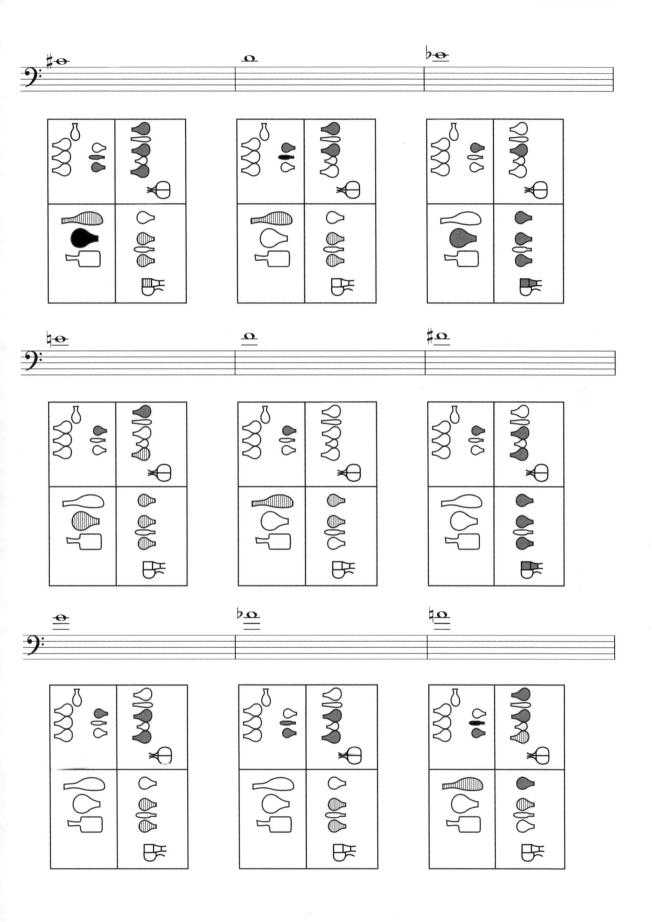

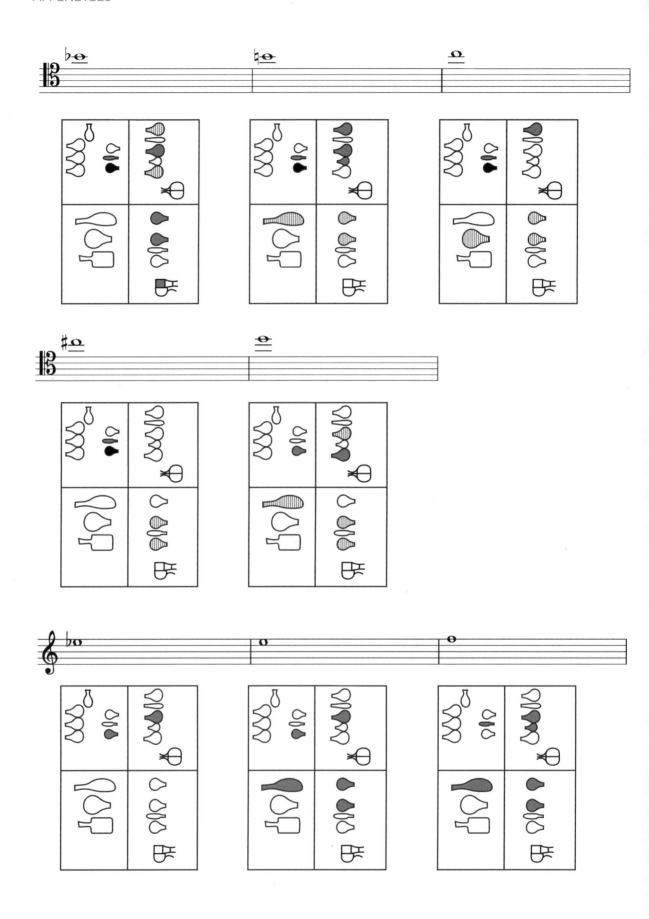

Auxiliary fingerings

These fingerings are useful for technical purposes in passages where the previous or following notes make it easier. They also help with some slurs. In the case of C# and D it can help with the cracks.

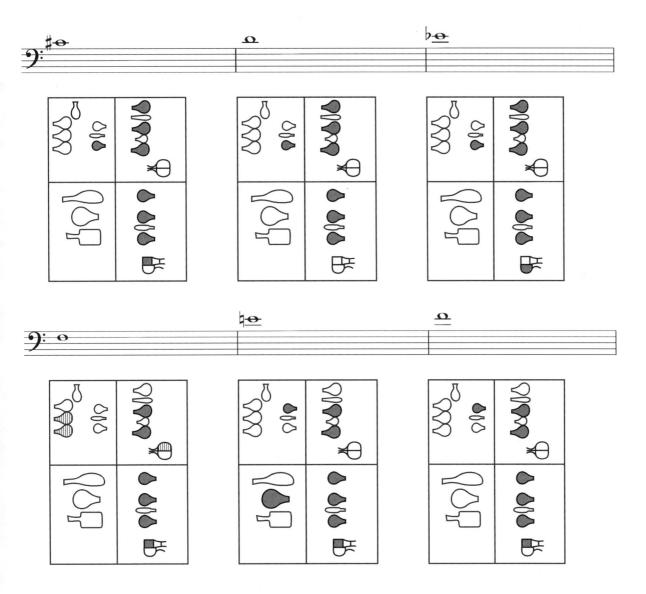

These fingerings provide a darker sound and can be very useful in legato, melodic phrases, and are very effective in soft dynamics.

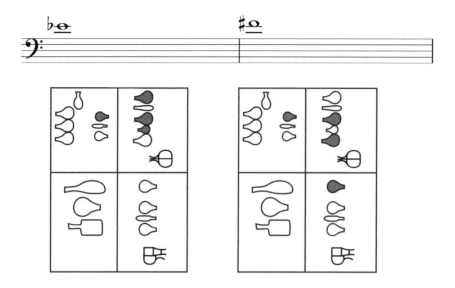

These fingerings are meant for mechanical easiness and easier flow.

Made in the USA
Columbia, SC
29 August 2024

41017849R00052